# MASS SHOOTINGS
# IN AMERICA

BY DUCHESS HARRIS, JD, PHD WITH JENNIFER SIMMS

**Essential Library**

An Imprint of Abdo Publishing | abdobooks.com

abdobooks.com

Published by Abdo Publishing, a division of ABDO, PO Box 398166, Minneapolis, Minnesota 55439. Copyright © 2019 by Abdo Consulting Group, Inc. International copyrights reserved in all countries. No part of this book may be reproduced in any form without written permission from the publisher. Essential Library™ is a trademark and logo of Abdo Publishing.

Printed in the United States of America, North Mankato, Minnesota
082018
012019

Cover Photo: John Locher/AP Images
Interior Photos: Rich Pedroncelli/AP Images, 4–5, 8; Ryan Rodrick Beiler/
Shutterstock Images, 12; AP Images, 14–15, 19; Matt Gentry/The Roanoke Times/
AP Images, 23; Michael Kitada/The Orange County Register/AP Images, 27;
Pablo Martinez Monsivais/AP Images, 28–29; David Giles/PA Wire URN:8948624/
Press Association/AP Images, 33; Rod McGuirk/AP Images, 35; Keith Homan/
Shutterstock Images, 36; Chuck Burton/AP Images, 38–39; iStockphoto, 43, 53, 75;
David Zalubowski/AP Images, 47; Alexandre MARCHI/Gamma-Rapho/Getty Images,
48–49; Gerald Herbert/AP Images, 55; Shutterstock Images, 58–59; Jay Janner/
Austin American-Statesman/AP Images, 64; David J. Phillip/AP Images, 69; Alex
Milan Tracy/Sipa USA/AP Images, 70–71; Mike Groll/AP Images, 73; Carlos Osorio/
AP Images, 78; Rachel Denny Clow/Corpus Christi Caller-Times/AP Images, 80–81;
Omar Ricardo Aquije/The Post-Star/AP Images, 85; Annie Rice/AP Images, 89;
Robyn Beck/AFP/Getty Images, 90–91; Ed Andrieski/AP Images, 94; Paul Morigi/AP
Images, 96

Editor: Alyssa Krekelberg
Series Designer: Maggie Villaume

Library of Congress Control Number: 2018948306

Publisher's Cataloging-in-Publication Data

Names: Harris, Duchess, author. | Simms, Jennifer, author.
Title: Mass shootings in America / by Duchess Harris and Jennifer Simms.
Description: Minneapolis, Minnesota : Abdo Publishing, 2019 | Series: Special
        reports set 4 | Includes online resources and index.
Identifiers: ISBN 9781532116780 (lib. bdg.) | ISBN 9781532159626 (ebook)
Subjects: LCSH: Mass shootings--Juvenile literature. | Firearms--Law and
        legislation--Juvenile literature. | Shootings in schools--Juvenile literature. |
        Mass public shootings--Juvenile literature.
Classification: DDC 364.15234--dc23

# CONTENTS

# CHAPTER ONE

# WHAT IS A MASS SHOOTING?

O n the morning of November 14, 2017, 44-year-old Kevin Neal was on a shooting rampage in Rancho Tehama, a small town in Northern California. He had already killed his wife and two neighbors before heading for Rancho Tehama Elementary, where a neighbor's seven-year-old son went to school.

Students and parents were gathered in the school's courtyard, waiting for the school day to begin. At approximately 7:50 a.m., staff members heard the loud pop of a gunshot nearby. Moments later, they heard two more gunshots. Immediately, the school secretary

Assistant Sheriff Phil Johnston of Tehama County discussed Kevin Neal's shooting with reporters.

jumped on the intercom and announced a school lockdown. Teachers rushed out and corralled children and parents into the building. Most of the people were safely inside when Neal charged into the school gates with a stolen pickup truck.

The school's custodian poked his head around the side of the building, drawing Neal's attention. At that moment, Neal's weapon appeared to jam, giving school officials the precious seconds needed to usher the remaining students inside. According to surveillance footage, approximately eight to ten seconds after all doors were locked, Neal aimed at the building and opened fire. Bullets pierced wood walls and windows. He tried repeatedly to access the kindergarten classroom and main office but could not get through.

In the community that day, five people were killed and 12 were injured.[1] At the school, one six-year-old boy was wounded. Thanks to quick medical

## WHERE MASS SHOOTINGS OCCUR

Although many people often associate schools with mass shootings, these events are much more likely to occur in business and government locations. According to a Federal Bureau of Investigation (FBI) study of active shooter events between 2000 and 2017, about 20 percent of active shooters targeted schools, whereas almost 75 percent occurred in other public locations.[2]

attention from staff, he was home from the hospital two weeks later. "I really truly believe that we would've had a horrific bloodbath in that school if that school hadn't taken the action when they did," said Assistant Tehama County Sheriff Phil Johnston.[3]

Since Colorado's Columbine High School shooting in 1999, lockdown drills have become commonplace in US schools. Students and staff practice securing themselves quickly in dark classrooms behind locked doors hoping to protect themselves from an armed gunman and prevent the next school massacre. Though some people may argue about the effectiveness of such drills, school officials in Rancho Tehama credit fast-acting staff members and a well-practiced lockdown procedure with saving lives.

Unfortunately, well-rehearsed drills and procedures aren't always enough to prevent a shooter from targeting students.

"THE LOCKDOWN PROCEDURE WAS IMPLEMENTED FLAWLESSLY. THE REASON THAT WE HAVE A SITUATION WHERE I HAVE ONE STUDENT INJURED ON CAMPUS AND NOTHING WORSE HAPPENING ON CAMPUS IS BECAUSE OF THE HEROIC ACTIONS OF ALL MEMBERS OF MY SCHOOL STAFF."[4]

—RICHARD FITZPATRICK, SUPERINTENDENT FOR CORNING UNION ELEMENTARY SCHOOL DISTRICT, INCLUDING RANCHO TEHAMA ELEMENTARY

Also, in public locations such as churches, concerts, or movie theaters, there are not always protocols for keeping patrons safe when a shooter attacks. Though Americans agree mass shootings are tragic events, much debate occurs about the best way to put an end to this phenomenon. All the while, the shootings continue.

## THE CHALLENGE OF DEFINING A MASS SHOOTING

There is no universal definition of the term *mass shooting*. Instead, the definition differs depending on who's

Employees at the Corning Union Elementary School District, of which Rancho Tehama Elementary is a part, listened to a news conference about the shooting.

counting and why. Horrific events such as what happened in the 2017 Las Vegas, Nevada, shooting—which left 58 dead and more than 500 injured—are universally considered mass shootings. But others, such as a 2017 church shooting in Antioch, Tennessee, which left one dead and seven injured, may or may not be considered mass shootings.[5]

A common definition of *mass shooting* is based on the definition of *mass murder* used by the Federal Bureau of Investigation (FBI): an incident in which four or more people are killed in a single event and location, not including the offender. Thus, many analysts and media outlets use the four-fatality rule when defining a *mass shooting*.

However, other groups use broader definitions. In 2013, the US Congress passed a law that defined *mass killings* as three or more people killed in a single incident. Mass shootings are a type of mass killing. Because of this, some people consider Congress's three-fatality rule as the federal

"WHILE THE DEFINITION OF A MASS SHOOTING MAY SEEM LIKE A FAIRLY TECHNICAL OR SEMANTIC DEBATE, IT HAS THE POWER TO DRIVE THE MEDIA NARRATIVE AND THE PUBLIC PERCEPTION OF THE SCOPE OF GUN VIOLENCE IN THE U.S."[6]

—CHRIS WILSON, JOURNALIST

## ACTIVE SHOOTERS

Since 2013, the FBI has favored the term *active shooter incidents* instead of the term *mass shootings*. According to the FBI, an *active shooter* is "one or more individuals actively engaged in killing or attempting to kill people in a populated area."[7] Instead of focusing on the number of casualties, this definition focuses on the intent of the shooter. Though the term *active shooter* is sometimes used as a synonym for *mass shooter*, the two are not the same. Only 40 percent of active shooters between 2000 and 2013 met the federal definition of *mass killer*, or someone who kills three or more people in a single incident.[8] As a result, FBI active shooter statistics can give the appearance that multiple-casualty mass shootings are more common than they really are.

definition of *mass shooting*. Still other people argue that a mass shooting shouldn't be defined by the number of fatalities alone. Instead, the shooter's motivation should be the determining factor. Some people believe that if the gunman intended to kill people at random, the event should be considered a mass shooting—even if no one actually died. Though most definitions of mass shooting focus on a shooter targeting people at random, others, such as the nonprofit research organization Gun Violence Archive, also count mass shootings that are motivated by terrorism, gang warfare, or domestic violence.

Because no universal definition or tracking of mass shootings exists, media outlets and organizations tend to pick the statistics that suit the message they are trying to convey. "Those who want to create a sense of crisis over the violence will tend to use lower cutoffs, while those who want to minimize the problem will use higher cutoffs," said Gary Kleck, criminology professor at Florida State University.[9]

For example, in a 2017 speech, US House minority leader Nancy Pelosi urged Congress to strengthen background checks days after the Las Vegas shooting. She said there had been 273 mass shootings in 2017.[10] The statistic she quoted came from Gun Violence Archive, which uses the broadest definition of *mass shooting*. In contrast, the political magazine *Mother Jones*, which keeps a database of shootings in which three or more people were killed, counted seven mass shootings in the same period.[11]

Without a common definition, it can be challenging for the average American to determine whether mass

## OVERALL GUN VIOLENCE A BIGGER PROBLEM THAN MASS SHOOTINGS

Though mass shootings routinely capture national attention, they represent a very small portion of gun violence in the United States. According to data from the Centers for Disease Control and Prevention (CDC), approximately 36,252 people died as a result of firearm use in 2015.[12] This number includes deaths related to crime, terrorism, gang warfare, domestic violence, suicide, and accidental shootings. In comparison, Gun Violence Archive, which uses the broadest definition of *mass shooting*, reported 475 mass shooting deaths that same year. One percent of gun deaths were related to mass shootings.[13]

shootings are on the rise and whether they present a real threat to public safety. As a result, in addition to statistics, it is useful to consider the history of mass shootings in the United States, examine the causes frequently blamed for these events, and compare the incidences of mass shootings in the United States to those experienced in other countries. By understanding the problem, people can develop solutions that may help prevent the next shooting.

## MASS SHOOTING OR TERRORIST ATTACK?

The random and unpredictable violence of mass shootings is often scary and unsettling to the public. Survivors of a shooting can feel terrorized by the event. But is a mass shooting a terrorist attack? Traditionally, the answer is no. Often, the gunman in a mass shooting is motivated by the desire to cause mass harm and chaos. However, a terrorist is typically motivated to cause harm and chaos to influence a government or further an ideology. Sometimes though, the lines between shooter and terrorist are blurry. For example, after the 2017 Las Vegas shooting, a social media debate broke out about whether to label the gunman as a domestic terrorist. Since the September 11, 2001, terrorist attack was carried out by Islamic extremists, many Americans imagine a terrorist to be only a Middle Eastern Muslim. However, terrorists can come from any country or practice any religion. Some people argued that if the shooter were Muslim, he would have been labeled a terrorist, but because he was white, he was not.

# CHAPTER TWO

# THE HISTORY
# OF MASS
# SHOOTINGS

he extensive media coverage regarding high-profile mass shootings can make it appear to people that mass shootings are a new and modern problem. However, the concept of mass violence and mass shootings is not new to the United States. In fact, these incidents have been occurring since the country's early history.

Mass shootings took place throughout the 1800s, though these events typically had fewer injuries and fatalities than shootings in the 2010s. Many of these shootings were specific, targeted acts of revenge,

Police officers have lost their lives during mass shooting events. One officer was killed during the University of Texas tower shooting in 1966.

but others showed the same indiscriminate violence of modern mass shootings. One example of this early violence occurred on March 30, 1891, when an unknown gunman fired into a crowd gathered for an end-of-school performance at the New Zion Church near Liberty, Mississippi. Fourteen people were wounded, some of them seriously.[1] The motive for the shooting was not reported.

## THE FIRST WAVE OF MASS KILLINGS

Historians note a spike in the number of mass murders, including shootings, from 1900 to 1939. Criminal researcher Grant Duwe refers to this period as the first wave of mass killings. During this time, the most common mass killings perpetrated by an individual, including mass shootings, happened between family members. This type of violence occurs when one member of the family, usually the father, murders other family members. In the 1920s and 1930s, this was particularly prevalent among white, rural farmers who had run into hard financial times due to the Great Depression. These killings were frequently committed from a misguided sense of love and the belief that death would spare family members from the pain of starvation and financial ruin.

Other shootings at the time were personal in nature and involved arguments between the shooter and the victim. In addition, some cases would fit the random nature of a modern mass shooting. An event such as that occurred in 1915 when a businessman with failing real estate developments opened fire in downtown Brunswick, Georgia, killing six and wounding 32.[2]

Between 1940 and 1966, the United States experienced a lull in mass killings and crime. Historians credit this lull to the national focus on World War II (1939–1945) and the boom in family and job security in the years afterward. However, this relative calm ended in 1966 with what is commonly considered by historians as the first modern mass shooting.

## SCHOOL BOMBER

One of the most notorious mass killings from the early 1900s took place in 1927 at a rural school in Bath, Michigan. The attacker was a school board member and the school's caretaker. On the day of the attack, he first killed his wife and then drove to the school, where he set hundreds of pounds of explosives in the school basement. At approximately 8:45 a.m., a bomb went off under one wing of the building. When the event was over, 44 people were dead.[3] Though not considered a mass shooting, the event remains the deadliest attack at a US school.

> "MASS MURDERERS HAVE FREQUENTLY BEEN DEPICTED AS LONERS IN BOTH THE POPULAR AND PROFESSIONAL LITERATURE. THE GROWING PREVALENCE OF MARRIAGE AND FAMILY DURING THE POSTWAR PERIOD MAY HAVE CURBED THE DELETERIOUS EFFECTS OF SOCIAL ISOLATION."[5]
>
> **—GRANT DUWE, AUTHOR OF *MASS MURDER IN THE UNITED STATES: A HISTORY***

# MODERN MASS SHOOTINGS (1966–1999)

The 1960s were a time of social and political unrest. Because of this factor, as well as a growing drug trade, crime began to rise throughout the nation. These changes paved the way for larger-scale crimes, including mass shootings. On August 1, 1966, a 25-year-old man, Charles Whitman, opened fire at the University of Texas, Austin. Perched in a prominent tower at the university, the gunman shot students walking across the grassy campus. In a span of 80 minutes, he injured more than 30 people. Seventeen people died from his attack.[4] Whitman was killed when police stormed the tower. The event became known as the University of Texas tower shooting.

Before the shooting spree, Whitman killed his mother and his wife. He also wrote a detailed suicide note, explaining he had uncontrollable violent thoughts. In the note, he urged investigators to do an autopsy on his body to determine the cause of his intense headaches.

After his death, a pathologist did find a brain tumor, and some doctors think it could have contributed to his mental instability. Other theories for the gunman's actions include growing up with a history of physical abuse, drug use, and mental illness. However, the precise motive behind the attack may never be known.

Unlike previous events, this shooting received a lot of media attention. Reporters covered the situation live from the scene, broadcasting images of the terrified crowd to viewers across the country. The story made headlines for weeks in local and national newspapers. Sometimes several articles about the event ran in the same paper in the same day, which had never happened with previous shootings.

First responders rushed a victim of the University of Texas tower shooting to a nearby ambulance.

Following the University of Texas tower shooting, other similar tragedies made national headlines through the 1960s and 1970s. The 1980s saw several high-profile workplace shootings. On August 20, 1986, part-time mail carrier Patrick Sherrill shot and killed 14 people at the Oklahoma post office where he had worked.[6] Sherrill was killed at the scene, but investigators believe his rampage was motivated by the criticism he had received from his supervisors about his quality of work.

One trend in the mass shootings that took place before 2000 was that they were committed predominately by adult white males. However, this all changed in the late 1990s when teens joined the fray. Starting in 1996, teens committed a handful of small-scale school shootings. Though some students were injured and one or two were killed, the events failed to gain the media attention of mass public shootings. But media focus on school shootings exploded when two teenagers

## GO POSTAL

The expression *go postal* is American slang that means to lose control, becoming angry and violent, usually from stress. It was coined in the 1990s after a string of post office shootings. The first of these shootings occurred in 1986 when disgruntled postal worker and ex-marine Patrick Sherrill stormed the Edmond, Oklahoma, post office, killing 14 and wounding six.[7]

opened fire at Columbine High School in Littleton, Colorado, on April 20, 1999, killing 13 people.[8] This event is considered a turning point in the history of mass shootings. Media coverage of the event lasted for months, and the name *Columbine* became synonymous in people's minds with the unthinkable tragedy.

## MASS SHOOTINGS IN THE 2000s

Mass shootings continued into the 2000s. After each tragedy, lawmakers debate the best way to prevent further shootings. Some suggest stricter gun control laws, whereas others want more funding for mental health programs or school safety. Sometimes new laws are passed. In other cases, groups that were affected by the tragedy, such as universities or school districts, implement new safety programs. But as of 2018, no change had been sweeping enough to prevent new mass shootings from occurring.

"THE TRAGEDY AT COLUMBINE WAS A WATERSHED EVENT AND WENT ON TO BECOME THE ARCHETYPAL MASS SHOOTING TO WHICH ALL OTHER SIMILAR EVENTS, LATER INCLUDING THOSE OUTSIDE OF SCHOOLS, WOULD BE COMPARED."[9]

—FROM *MASS SHOOTINGS: MEDIA, MYTHS, AND REALITIES* BY JACLYN SCHILDKRAUT AND H. JAYMI ELSASS

However, the 2007 shooting at Virginia Tech—a university in Blacksburg, Virginia—is an example of a tragedy that prompted change. On April 16, Seung-Hui Cho shot and killed 32 people before killing himself.[10] At the time, it was the deadliest mass shooting in US history. This event brought about improved notification systems to warn college students of emergency situations on campus. On the morning of the tragedy, Cho initially shot two students in a dorm.[11] Approximately two hours later, he chained shut the doors of a university building and continued his killing spree. Students and faculty didn't receive an email about the first shooting, though, until approximately the same time Cho began his second wave of killing. If warnings had been sent out sooner, officials believe many lives could have been saved.

Police officers raced to the Virginia Tech campus after the shooting began.

In the 2010s, the severity of mass shootings increased. One mass shooting occurred at Sandy Hook Elementary School in Newtown, Connecticut, on December 14, 2012. Twenty-year-old Adam Lanza shot his way through the front office and killed 20 first graders and six staff members before killing himself.[13] This tragedy renewed the efforts of school districts to improve campus safety, especially for middle schools and elementary schools. As a result of Sandy Hook, many safety upgrades are now commonplace in US schools, including buzzer systems at entrances and interior doors that lock automatically. Lockdown drills and active shooter drills occur regularly for all grade levels, and armed school resource officers are more common, even in elementary schools.

The June 12, 2016, tragedy at a gay nightclub in Orlando, Florida, sparked a discussion about police response to a shooting. During the attack, Omar Mateen killed 49 people and injured many others.[14] The nightclub, Pulse, was popular among the LGBTQ community, and this community was heavily affected by the shooting. Though police responded promptly to the event, they were not trained on how to deal with a terrorist or hostage situation. Typically, that training is reserved for the police force's special weapons and tactics (SWAT) teams. But regular police are usually the first on the scene. As a result, experts recommend all police receive training on how to best respond to a shooting.

As of August 2018, the largest mass shooting in US history was the Las Vegas shooting. The event took place on October 1, 2017, at the Mandalay Bay Resort and Casino. The gunman, Stephen Paddock, shot and killed 58 people and injured more than 500 people at an outdoor concert.[15] He fired on the crowd

## ARE MASS SHOOTINGS AN EPIDEMIC?

It is clear from history that mass shootings are not a new phenomenon. But many news headlines from the 2000s call the modern wave of mass shootings an epidemic. Criminal researcher Grant Duwe doesn't agree. According to Duwe, there has not been a real increase in the number of mass shootings that take place each year, but there has been an increase in the number of victims killed and injured at each event. He believes that although mass shootings are not more frequent, they have become more severe.

from his hotel room window using rifles modified with a bump stock—an attachment that makes a semiautomatic gun fire automatically with only one press of the trigger. Before police could enter his hotel room, Paddock shot and killed himself.

As a result of the tragedy, hotels were forced to rethink how they manage security for their guests. However, perhaps the biggest challenge for preventing another tragedy such as this one is stopping shooters before they can commit any crime. In Paddock's case, he gave off almost no warning signs before the attack. And after much investigation, authorities were not able to determine what motivated Paddock to attack.

## TYPES OF GUNS

The three main types of guns are rifles, shotguns, and handguns. A rifle is a high-powered, long-barreled gun. Certain types of rifles are used by the military. Other types may be legal for civilian use. A shotgun is often used for hunting and target shooting. The main difference between a rifle and a shotgun is the barrel. Shotgun barrels are straight, whereas rifle barrels are rifled, meaning spiraled, to help improve their accuracy. Handguns, also called pistols, are smaller with shorter barrels and can be used with one hand. They are used by police officers and by civilians who want an easy-to-conceal weapon.

# FROM THE
# HEADLINES

## FINANCIAL RELIEF
## FOR VICTIMS

Reports of mass shooting victims often focus on the people killed, especially when the number of casualties is high. However, people who are injured often face lifelong physical challenges. In addition, those who witness the event may experience emotional health consequences. Recovering physically and mentally from a mass shooting can be expensive. There are no government assistance programs to help shooting victims. Instead, victims rely on their own insurance and donations from privately run funds to fill in the gaps.

For example, the Las Vegas Victims Fund, a nonprofit organization, distributed millions of dollars to victims who applied for assistance. A similar fund was created after the Orlando nightclub shooting. However, the money raised was not enough to cover the estimated amount in actual costs. These costs include things such as medical expenses, lost wages, and changes to quality of life. And some people, such as Las Vegas shooting witness Christine Caria, didn't receive help because their applications for assistance were not approved.

Friends and family of the Las Vegas shooting victims mourned after the tragedy.

Though Carla wasn't shot, she sustained a back injury when she was trampled by the fleeing crowd. Her pain medication caused her to have a seizure, which affected her memory. She also had to close her boot-accessory business because setting up her booth at festivals was too traumatizing. However, Carla is ineligible to receive money from the victims' fund because she didn't seek treatment for her injuries right away.

# CHAPTER THREE

# AN AMERICAN
# PROBLEM?

There is a perception that mass shootings are predominately an American problem. As President Barack Obama explained, "We Americans are not an inherently more violent people than folks in other countries. . . . The main difference that sets our nation apart, what makes us so susceptible to so many mass shootings, is that we don't do enough—we don't take the basic common-sense actions to keep guns out of the hands of criminals and dangerous people. What's different in America is that it's easy to get your hands on a gun."[1]

The United States gives its citizens the right to bear arms in the Second Amendment to the US Constitution. The American public has more guns per person than

In 2016, President Barack Obama and Vice President Joe Biden visited the memorial site for the Orlando nightclub shooting victims.

any other developed country. Though the US population makes up 5 percent of the global population, the country has produced 31 percent of the world's mass shooters.[2]

But mass shootings are a global phenomenon. University of Alabama professor Adam Lankford has studied mass shootings worldwide since the University of Texas tower shooting. According to his research, deadly shootings take place in other countries as well. As of mid-2018, the deadliest shooting worldwide took place in 2011 in Norway. And of the top ten worst mass shootings worldwide, seven took place in countries other than the United States.[3] Lankford's data set excludes shootings that were clearly motivated by terrorism.

## RATE OF GUN OWNERSHIP

"A nation's civilian firearm ownership rate is the strongest predictor of its number of public mass shooters," said researcher Adam Lankford, explaining the results of his 2015 study of mass shootings worldwide. His study examined incidents from 1966 to 2012. Lankford found five of the top 15 countries for mass shootings per capita—the United States, Yemen, Switzerland, Finland, and Serbia—also had the highest rates of gun ownership in the world.[4]

## REDUCING GUN VIOLENCE

Though mass shootings take place worldwide, some countries have successfully decreased their number of

# MORE TO THE
# STORY

## THE DEADLIEST MASS SHOOTING

The deadliest mass shooting in Europe took place in Norway on July 22, 2011. A 33-year-old gunman detonated a fertilizer bomb in the city of Oslo, killing eight people. Then, dressed in a police uniform, he took a short ferry ride to a camp on the island of Utøya, where he opened fire on the teenage campers. Sixty-seven people died on the island, and an additional two died later at the hospital. Approximately one hour after the shooting began, the gunman surrendered to police. A CBS article cited multiple motivations for the shooting, including the shooter saying he had been inspired by a terrorist group. After standing trial, the gunman was sentenced to 21 years in prison—the maximum possible sentence Norway allows.[5] However, if he is considered a threat at the time he is due for release, his sentence can be extended.

annual gun-related deaths. In the United Kingdom, Germany, and Australia, past mass shootings served as the catalyst for significant government policy changes that worked to curb the gun violence.

The United Kingdom's gun control laws are some of the strictest in the world. In response to a 1987 shooting that killed 16 people, the government passed the Firearms Act. This act banned high-powered, semiautomatic firearms such as the ones used in the attack. However, despite the regulations, a gunman with handguns killed 16 preschool-aged children and their teacher at Dunblane Primary School in Scotland in 1996.[6] After that, the Firearms Act was amended to ban all citizens from owning handguns. After the act was revised, the only people who could lawfully own handguns in the United Kingdom were police, military, and select citizens, such as security guards. In addition, hunters and target shooters can seek the government's permission to own shotguns. Shooting clubs can also apply to own guns for their members to use at the club.

In Germany, guns are not banned like they are in the United Kingdom, but they are carefully controlled. In 2002,

The 1996 school shooting in Scotland is known as the Dunblane Primary School massacre.

a school shooter killed 16 people in Erfurt, Germany.[7] In response, the country passed a law that restricted young people's access to large-caliber weapons and strengthened regulations for safe gun storage. After another school shooting in 2009, the country also created a national gun registry. Since then, the country has experienced only one other mass shooting, which took place in 2016.

In 1996, a shooting in the Australian tourist town of Port Arthur left 35 people dead and 18 injured.[8] The event prompted the nation's government to nationalize gun control laws and ban all semiautomatic weapons. It also instituted a buyback program, reimbursing citizens for turning in their guns. Then, in 2002, when a shooter killed two people and injured five others with a handgun, the government added a separate handgun bill and buyback program.[9] Since the 2002 incident, there hadn't been another mass shooting in Australia as of mid-2018. In addition, gun violence and gun suicides had declined dramatically.

## SWITZERLAND: HIGH GUN OWNERSHIP, LOW GUN CRIME

In some countries, tighter national restrictions on guns led to decreases in mass shootings and gun violence. However, it is possible for a country with high levels of gun ownership to have low gun violence. Switzerland has the third-highest rate of gun ownership in the world. Like the United States, the country has a strong tradition of gun ownership. In Switzerland, this tradition is spurred by the required military service of men ages 18 to 34, along with the popularity of hunting and shooting contests. Yet, the Swiss have not experienced a mass shooting since 2001.

The difference is likely the result of several factors. Though it is relatively easy to buy guns in both Switzerland

A memorial was constructed in Tasmania, Australia, to remember the victims of the Port Arthur shooting.

Many US states don't demand background checks on people who buy firearms from unlicensed dealers at gun shows.

and the United States, Switzerland has universal, mandatory background checks, whereas the United States does not. The Swiss also have many regulations for how a gun must be safely stored and transported. In addition, children as young as 12 are trained to handle guns safely and responsibly. Though there are a significant number of firearms in Switzerland, the number of gun deaths remains low—approximately one firearm death per 200,000 people in 2010. In comparison, the United States' rate in the same year was approximately ten firearm deaths per 200,000 people.[10]

Though mass shootings continue to be a problem in the United States and around the world, countries such as the United Kingdom prove that strict gun policies can reduce gun violence. In contrast, Switzerland proves that a country's citizens can own guns yet ward off mass shootings with a strong culture of gun safety and responsibility.

"ONE OF THE REASONS THE CRIME RATE IN SWITZERLAND IS LOW DESPITE THE PREVALENCE OF WEAPONS . . . IS THE CULTURE OF RESPONSIBILITY AND SAFETY THAT IS ANCHORED IN SOCIETY AND PASSED FROM GENERATION TO GENERATION."[11]

**—HELENA BACHMANN, JOURNALIST**

# CHAPTER FOUR

# PROFILE OF
# A SHOOTER

**A**fter a mass shooting takes place, investigators and reporters scramble to understand the shooter, trying to determine what would motivate a person to commit such a horrific act. Because the majority of mass shooters die at the scene, investigators are often left trying to piece together a profile, or a description, of the gunman. In some cases, investigators discover similarities between shooters. However, in most aspects the gunmen are quite diverse. As a result, it is hard for researchers to create a reliable profile of a shooter.

In 2015, Dylann Roof killed nine black churchgoers in Charleston, South Carolina. He was later sentenced to death.

# DEMOGRAPHICS

Mass shooters represent a wide range of ages. Since 1966, the youngest shooter was an 11-year-old middle schooler who opened fire on his classmates. The oldest was Paddock, the Las Vegas shooter, who was a 64-year-old retiree. However, the majority of shooters are working-age adults, with a median age of 33.

One common belief is that mass shooters are predominately white—and they are. According to *Mother Jones*, which tracks shootings in which three or more people are killed, 54 percent of gunmen from 1982 to 2017 have been white. In that same period, 16 percent of mass shooters were black.[1] In addition, a small percentage of mass shooters have been Hispanic, Asian, or Native American.

## FEMALE SHOOTERS

Whichever guidelines a person uses to count mass shootings, a very small number of mass shooters have been women. One was a mail carrier who shot a former neighbor and six employees at a mail processing facility in Goleta, California, in 2006. Another was a woman who killed her brother and three others in Alturas, California, in 2014. A third was a mother who partnered with her husband in San Bernardino, California, to murder 14 people at a center for people with developmental disabilities in 2016.[2]

There is one trait that shooters have in common: they are almost always men. Using the data on mass shootings from the *Washington Post*, which uses the four-fatality rule, only three of the 153 shooters between 1966 and 2018 have been women.[3]

# WEAPONS OF CHOICE

When a mass murder is the goal, guns are the weapon of choice for mass killers. This is because guns can inflict a high amount of damage in a short amount of time. Some shooters carry multiple weapons. Of the 298 guns used in mass shootings between 1966 and mid-2018, 168 were purchased legally and 52 were obtained illegally. Investigators were unable to determine how the remaining 78 guns were obtained.[4] The most common type of weapon used in mass shootings is the 9mm semiautomatic handgun. It was used by the Virginia Tech shooter in 2007. However, since a ban on assault weapons was lifted in 2004, semiautomatic rifles such as the AR-15 have been used more often in recent shootings with high fatalities. Semiautomatic assault-style rifles were used in the Newtown, Orlando, and Las Vegas shootings.

# SHOOTERS' MOTIVATIONS

When a shooting takes place, people often ask why. Though the reasons are complicated, varied, or sometimes impossible to know, certain trends surface. One common motivation is revenge. The gunman may feel the need to get back at a specific person, such as a romantic partner or former boss. He may target a group of people at a former workplace or school. Or he may feel a general need for revenge on society that would prompt him to shoot strangers in a public location.

Mass killers are often portrayed as loners—people who choose to exist on the fringes of society. But Katherine Newman, a sociologist at

## IS THE AR-15 AN ASSAULT RIFLE?

The AR-15 rifle is commonly blamed for mass shootings. It is a lightweight, semiautomatic version of the military's M-16 rifle. Originally produced by Armalite (AR stands for Armalite Rifle) in the 1950s, versions of this rifle are now sold by multiple gun manufacturers. The National Rifle Association (NRA) estimates there are more than 15 million of these types of guns in the United States.[5] Though many people, including the federal government, consider the AR-15 an assault rifle, the gun industry argues the term is incorrect. It defines an *assault rifle* as a military rifle with select capabilities, meaning the user can switch between automatic and semiautomatic firing modes. In contrast, the AR-15 is only a semiautomatic gun and fires like other civilian sport rifles. However, because the AR-15 looks like a military assault rifle and has been used in high-profile shootings such as Sandy Hook, many gun control advocates believe it should be banned.

Gun control advocates have pushed for a semiautomatic rifle ban.

Johns Hopkins University, says that view is not quite accurate. Indeed, after a shooting, people will often come forward to say they had been friends with the shooter. Instead, Newman believes the shooters struggle with social integration. Mass shooters may have a hard time connecting with others—they struggle to fit in. They feel isolated, even when it's not always true, or lonely.

Psychologist Peter Langman, who has done extensive research on school shooters, helps the public understand their motives by breaking them into three categories. The first group he calls the traumatized shooter—someone who was inspired to act because he had been the victim of abuse and ongoing trauma. The next group he calls

## STRAIN THEORY: WHY SHOOTERS SNAP

Researchers Jack Levin and Eric Madfis have created a theory to explain why people become shooters. This idea, called Strain Theory, describes the increasing levels of stress that lead an individual to snap. In stage one, the individual experiences a long-term strain. In stage two, the strain is uncontrolled and the individual doesn't have the resources to help him deal with it. In stage three, a specific triggering event, such as a loss or setback, sparks the idea of a shooting. In stage four, the individual begins to plan, and in stage five, he attacks. These stages suggest that the motivation to commit mass murder develops over time instead of happening suddenly.

psychopathic. These gunmen are cold and callous, focused on only themselves. The third he calls psychotic, or having a genuine mental health disorder that would allow someone to be social and likable on the outside but live in a fantasy world of death and murder on the inside.

When a mass shooter goes on a rampage, some people in the media are quick to label the person as having a mental illness. How, they ask, could a person kill random strangers unless there was something wrong with his brain function? However, it can be very difficult to determine whether a shooter truly suffered from mental illness—especially if that person dies during the attack.

Criminologists James Alan Fox and Emma Fridel analyzed mass shootings in which four or more people were killed between 1966 and 2015. They found that only 14.8 percent of shooters had been diagnosed with a psychotic disorder, a condition such as schizophrenia, that disrupts normal brain function.[6] However, not all shooters with mental illness have visited a medical professional and received a diagnosis.

According to criminal researcher Duwe, the percentage of shooters with mental illness may be much higher. In his review of current and past shootings, Duwe found that 59 percent of gunmen from 1900 to 2017 showed signs of serious mental illness prior to the attack. He also found that only one-third of these people sought mental health treatment before the shooting event.[7]

Finally, a common assumption is that mass shooters always commit suicide or are killed by law enforcement. Of the 155 shooters included in the

## LINK TO DOMESTIC VIOLENCE

Some evidence suggests that people who commit domestic violence are more likely to commit mass murder. Research compiled by Everytown for Gun Safety, a nonprofit that supports gun control, found approximately 57 percent of shooters between 2009 and 2015 also killed a present or former spouse or other family members during their rampage. They also found that 16 percent of shooters had been previously charged with domestic violence. "Having a history of violence might help neutralize the natural barriers to committing violence," said Paul Gill, a lecturer at University College London.[8]

> "IT IS IMPORTANT TO REMEMBER THAT ONLY A VERY SMALL PERCENTAGE OF VIOLENT ACTS ARE COMMITTED BY PEOPLE WHO ARE DIAGNOSED WITH, OR IN TREATMENT FOR, MENTAL ILLNESS."[11]
>
> —JESSICA HENDERSON DANIEL, PRESIDENT OF THE AMERICAN PSYCHOLOGICAL ASSOCIATION

*Washington Post* data set, 88—or 57 percent—died at the scene. That means the other 43 percent were apprehended at the scene or escaped.[9] Those shooters who did survive and were captured faced trials and prison sentences. The gunman at the 2012 Aurora, Colorado, theater shooting received 12 life sentences—one for each of the people he killed—plus 3,318 years in prison for injuring other victims and for putting together explosive devices that he left in his apartment.[10]

The Colorado theater shooter attacked people during the midnight showing of *The Dark Knight Rises*.

# CHAPTER FIVE

# US CULTURE AND MASS SHOOTERS

**W**hen a mass shooting occurs, people find a multitude of things to blame. Politicians and the media are often quick to blame the tragedy on the shooter's personality or mental state. Other people blame things that influenced the shooter, such as an obsession with violent video games. Still others blame US culture, citing male stereotypes or the way the media portrays violence.

## VIOLENT VIDEO GAMES

After the Sandy Hook shooting in 2012, President Obama spoke about a possible link between violent

Violent video games are often targeted by politicians as a reason for mass shootings.

video games and mass shootings. The gunman, it was reported, was an avid gamer. Obama asked Congress to "fund research into the effects that violent video games have on young minds."[1] This sentiment was echoed in 2018 after the Parkland, Florida, shooting. This shooting occurred at Marjory Stoneman Douglas (MSD) High School, and 17 people were killed.[2] President Donald Trump called a meeting with representatives of the video game industry to discuss the effects of violent games on the country's youth. In fact, people's perceptions of the link between mass shootings and violent gaming goes back to the Columbine shooting, when it was reported that the shooters spent copious hours playing *Doom*—a first-person shooter game.

Some research, such as a 2010 study by Iowa State University professor Craig A. Anderson, shows that playing violent video games does increase aggressive behavior in gamers. However, as Mark Appelbaum, a professor from the University of California, points out, there is a big leap between feeling aggression and committing a crime. Other research, such as a 2018 study from the University of New York, suggests there is no link between playing violent video games and being more violent in real life. In addition, a study by psychologist Patrick Markey found that only 20 percent of school shooters played violent video games.[4] In contrast, 70 percent of high schoolers reported playing these games.[5]

Despite the research, many people still believe there is a clear link between video games and violence. Wayne LaPierre, the executive vice president for the National Rifle Association (NRA)—which supports gun rights—said after the Sandy Hook shooting, "There exists in this country, sadly, a callous, corrupt, and corrupting shadow industry that sells and stows violence against its own people through vicious, violent video games."[6] However, critics claim the reason that

## THE LACK OF A LINK

A 2015 study published in *Psychology of Popular Media and Culture* aimed to discover the link between violent video games and violent crime. Researchers examined crime rates in the months following the release of popular violent video games and found that violent crime did not increase. In some cases, violent crime actually went down. One possible explanation for this trend is that those with aggressive or violent tendencies may experience a release by playing the game, making them less likely to act out these behaviors in real life.

groups such as the NRA blame video games is that they want to distract the conversation from gun reform.

## CULTURE OF MALE VIOLENCE

Researcher Jackson Katz doesn't blame mass shootings on violent video games, and he doesn't blame them on guns. Instead, he says there's only one culprit for the prevalence of violence in the United States: men. According to Katz, the maleness of this problem often gets overlooked by the media because men are seen as the dominant gender group. He believes that if the majority of shooters were overwhelmingly female, there would be a national conversation about gender and violence, but because they are male, there is not. However, Katz and other experts believe this conversation about male gender and violence is exactly what the United States needs to curb mass shootings.

After all, it's not just mass shootings that are a predominately male problem. Men commit the vast majority of violent crimes. According

"WOMEN LOSE JOBS. WOMEN FEEL NEGLECTED BY THEIR LOVED ONES. WOMEN ARE ROMANTICALLY REJECTED. WOMEN, AS A RULE, DO NOT RESPOND BY SHOOTING UP SCHOOLS OR WORKPLACES."[7]

—JENNIFER WRIGHT, WRITER FOR *HARPER'S BAZAAR*

In the United States, men own more guns than women do, which increases the potential for men to commit gun violence.

to FBI statistics, men commit 89 percent of murders, 99 percent of rapes, and 87 percent of robberies.[8]

According to Katz, the reason men are more violent than women is due to the masculine male stereotype. Researchers Rachel Kalish and Michael Kimmel compare this stereotype to Western movies: the lone gunman taking the law into his own hands and exacting revenge. They say men in the United States are taught through male role models and the media that they must be tough and aggressive loners, and that this "toxic masculinity" is the catalyst for violent action.[9] Because of this stereotype, men feel they are expected, even entitled, to respond to stress or disappointment—such as losing a job or being rejected by a romantic partner—with violence.

In addition, this masculine stereotype may prevent men who truly do have mental health issues from seeking help for fear of being considered weak. This is especially problematic in light of research that says women who suffer from depression tend to take their anger inward, whereas men with depression explode with violent rage. As a result, these researchers suggest Americans should openly discuss society's expectations of masculinity and what can be done to help men deal with negative emotions in a healthy way.

## MASS SHOOTINGS CAUSE MORE MASS SHOOTINGS

In 2015, Malcom Gladwell, a writer for the *New Yorker*, wrote an article theorizing that mass shootings can spread like a disease. His thought was that one mass shooting event can infect people with the idea to carry out their own shooting rampage. Like an avalanche, small, isolated events inspire more frequent and more violent events until even the most stable people can get carried away in the slide.

After the MSD High School shooting, the media attention helped student advocates push for gun control.

According to criminal researcher Duwe, there has not been a significant increase in the frequency of mass shootings in the last several years. However, there has been an increase in the violence of each event. "If we look at say the top seven in terms of how deadly they've been, five of the seven deadliest have been in the last ten years," Duwe said in a 2017 interview with NBC shortly after the Sutherland Springs church shooting claimed 26 lives. And if each of these events is seen as a role model for future shooters,

"IF IT SEEMS LIKE THE SHOOTINGS ARE BECOMING MORE FREQUENT, IT MIGHT BE BECAUSE MASS MURDER CAN CATCH ON LIKE AN EPIDEMIC."[10]

—DEREK THOMPSON, WRITER FOR THE *ATLANTIC*

then, "America has more potentially deadly role models," Duwe explained.[11] In addition, a 2015 report from the University of Arizona shows the tendency for a clustering of mass shootings to occur closely after a single event.

In the case of a disease, the virus spreads from person to person. In the case of violence, the epidemic spreads through the media. When extensive media coverage is given to a shooting, other potential shooters get the idea to try the same thing. In addition, the media coverage gives an element of fame to mass shooters. Some, such as Columbine shooters Harris and Klebold, even become household names. For a person suffering from rejection or lacking the ability to connect, this instant fame, or infamy, can be very attractive.

As a result, *Mother Jones* offered suggestions to the media for more responsible coverage of mass shootings. One suggestion is the no-name rule, which encourages

## NO NOTORIETY CAMPAIGN

Tom Teves lost his son, Alex, in the 2012 Aurora theater shooting. The day after the shooting, Teves helped launch the No Notoriety campaign. The campaign asks the media not to focus on the shooter but instead focus on the victims, heroes, and survivors of the event. The suggested policies have been officially adopted by *People* magazine and the Florida chapter of the Society of Professional Journalists.

reporters to limit the use of the shooter's name. Another is to limit photos of the shooter, especially any posed photos the shooter may have purposefully left behind. The theory is if being a mass shooter gets little publicity, then there won't be as many copycats, slowing the spread of the violence epidemic.

## SHOOTER FASCINATED BY INFAMY

The shooter who killed nine people at Umpqua Community College in Oregon in 2015 was fascinated with other famous shooters.[12] He posted online that he admired the infamy of the disgruntled man who'd shot and killed two former coworkers on live television a few months prior. "A man who was known by no one, is now known by everyone," wrote the shooter. "His face splashed across every screen, his name across the lips of every person on the planet, all in the course of one day. Seems the more people you kill, the more you're in the limelight."[13]

# CHAPTER SIX

# THE GUN
# DEBATE

There is one thing all mass shootings have in common: they are committed by people with a gun, and sometimes several guns. As a result, the conversation on how to prevent further mass shootings frequently turns to gun laws. People in favor of gun control argue it's the easy access to guns that makes mass shootings possible. They note that with stricter gun laws, future tragedies could be prevented.

Those in favor of gun rights argue that it's not the guns that commit the crimes but rather the people behind the guns. They believe that public policy needs to focus on the human factor rather than the weapons. With strong opinions on both sides, few legal changes have been made even as mass shootings

In 2018, demonstrators organized a "lie-in" outside the White House to encourage gun control.

become more severe. Instead, the debate continues with passionate arguments on either side.

# GUN CONTROL

Americans have the right to own firearms, as protected by the Second Amendment. Therefore, it is unlikely that gun ownership in the United States will ever become as legally restricted as it is in other countries such as the United Kingdom. As a result, gun control advocates focus their attention on better regulating who can buy guns and what types of firearms they can legally own.

One common request by gun control advocates is for universal background checks. A federal law mandates that all federally licensed gun dealers perform background checks on gun buyers. These checks determine whether the buyer has a criminal record or history of mental illness that would disqualify him or her from buying a gun. But laws about background checks for other types of gun sales differ by state. Some states require them for all gun purchases. Other states don't require them if the gun is purchased at a gun show or bought secondhand. An estimated 20 percent of guns are bought without

# MORE TO THE
# STORY

## THE SECOND AMENDMENT DEBATE

The Second Amendment states, "A well regulated Militia, being necessary to the security of a free State, the right of the people to keep and bear Arms, shall not be infringed." The antiquated and awkward phrasing of this amendment has left Americans arguing over its meaning for decades. Those in favor of gun rights read the phrase "the right of the people to keep and bear Arms" and interpret it as a constitutional guarantee of the people's right to own weapons. In contrast, those in favor of gun control point to the phrase "A well regulated Militia" and argue that the framers of the Constitution were focused on providing for organized armed forces, not individuals. The Constitution is interpreted when it's tested in court, and for years the courts leaned in favor of the "Militia" interpretation. However, in 2008, the Supreme Court made a significant shift toward gun ownership when it struck down a handgun ban in Washington, DC. The court claimed the law infringed on Americans' rights to own guns for protection, emphasizing the individual's right to own firearms.

## THE BRADY BILL

In November 1993, President Bill Clinton signed the Brady Handgun Violence Prevention Act. The bill was named after Jim Brady, press secretary to President Ronald Reagan, who was shot and seriously injured in a 1983 assassination attempt. The bill introduced a system of background checks for federally licensed gun dealers. The Brady Campaign to End Gun Violence, a nonprofit advocacy group named in honor of Brady, estimates the sale of more than three million guns has been blocked as a result of this law, keeping guns out of the hands of dangerous people such as convicted felons.[4]

background checks through these loopholes.[2] As a result, it's still easy for guns to get into the hands of people who shouldn't have them.

Another gun control argument is for stricter regulations on the sale of ammunition, both who can buy it and how much they can purchase. Supporters of this regulation argue that controlling ammunition sales may stop someone who owns a gun illegally from being able to use it. In addition, they argue that high-capacity magazines should be banned because they make it easier for a mass shooter to do more damage before reloading. Reporters for *Mother Jones* examined 62 mass shootings from 1982 to 2012 and found that 50 percent of shooters used high-capacity magazines.[3]

Gun control advocates also recommend limiting the purchase of military-style, semiautomatic weapons that can do the most damage. Their logic is that although all guns can kill people, some guns kill more than others. Semiautomatic rifles, such as the AR-15, have been used at many of the deadliest attacks in the United States. Such weapons were actually banned in the United States from 1994 to 2004. Proponents believe reinstating the ban would save lives in the case of an attack.

## GUN RIGHTS

People who support gun rights believe additional gun laws are not necessary. Instead, they argue that a well-armed society is a safer society. LaPierre said in an interview after Sandy Hook, "The only way to stop a bad guy with a gun is a good guy with a gun."[5] LaPierre and other gun advocates believe armed civilians have the power to step in and prevent crime, terrorism, and mass shootings from occurring. They cite examples such as a 2007 shooting at New Life Church in Colorado Springs, which was stopped when a volunteer security guard shot and killed the attacker.

"IN RETROSPECT SANDY HOOK MARKED THE END OF THE US GUN CONTROL DEBATE. ONCE AMERICA DECIDED KILLING CHILDREN WAS BEARABLE, IT WAS OVER."[6]

—DAN HODGES, A
BRITISH JOURNALIST

Some Second Amendment supporters don't agree with the idea of using gun violence victims to advocate for gun control.

Another argument for gun ownership is expressed in a common NRA saying: "Guns don't kill people. People kill people."[7] The idea behind this argument is that the guns aren't to blame. Instead, it's the people using them that are the problem. As a result, gun rights advocates argue that factors other than guns, such as a culture of violence in society or the lack of treatment for mental health issues, are the real problems. By putting the blame on guns, they believe the cultural factors that inspire shootings remain ignored.

Another common argument is that gun control won't stop

"BANNING GUNS ISN'T THE ANSWER TO PREVENTING VIOLENCE ANY MORE THAN BANNING CARS WOULD BE THE ANSWER TO PREVENTING PEOPLE FROM BEING KILLED IN CAR ACCIDENTS."[8]

—VICKY HARTZLER, REPUBLICAN US REPRESENTATIVE FROM MISSOURI

people intent on committing violent acts. As gun rights advocate John R. Lott Jr. said, "The problem with such [gun control] laws is that they take away guns from law-abiding citizens, while would-be criminals ignore them."[9] Gun advocates say that criminals will either find a way to obtain guns illegally or devise another way to cause destruction, such as by creating a bomb. And, advocates argue, when regular citizens can't own guns, they can't protect themselves against the people who do have them.

## LACK OF FUNDING FOR GUN RESEARCH

No one knows for sure what approach would be best for preventing gun violence in the United States. There is little research done on gun deaths compared with other leading causes of death in the United

## GUNS AND SELF-DEFENSE

One main gun rights argument is that Americans need guns for self-defense. However, a Harvard University study found that guns are used to stop only approximately 0.9 percent of crimes. "The average person . . . has basically no chance in their lifetime ever to use a gun in self-defense," said David Hemenway, the lead researcher on the study.[10] According to gun control organization Brady Campaign to End Gun Violence, guns are used more frequently for other purposes. For each time a gun is used in self-defense, guns are used in 11 completed and attempted suicides, seven criminal assaults or homicides, and four accidental injuries or deaths.[11] As a result, Hemenway and other experts argue that the risks of owning a gun far outweigh the protection it might provide.

States. For example, the US government spends $1,000 in research for every traffic fatality but only $63 per every gun death.[12] This is because the federal government has prevented government organizations from doing this type of gun research.

In 1996, the NRA pushed Congress to pass the Dickey Amendment. This amendment prohibited the Centers for Disease Control and Prevention (CDC) from spending money on research that could find results that might promote gun control. This amendment left national agencies such as the CDC, which typically researches causes of accidental death, unable to do gun research. In addition, a 2003 bill prevented the Bureau of Alcohol, Tobacco, Firearms and Explosives from releasing data on where guns are bought and sold. Instead, gun research is done by small, privately funded organizations. There are not enough studies to pave the way for gun policy change.

## THE MAJORITY OF AMERICANS SUPPORT GUN LAW CHANGE

The majority of Americans think gun laws should change. A 2018 survey by Quinnipiac University, conducted shortly after the MSD High School shooting, found 97 percent of US voters and 97 percent of gun owners support universal background checks for gun purchases. In addition, it found that 67 percent of Americans supported a ban on assault-style weapons.[13]

But even if Americans favor more gun control, citizens cannot change gun laws directly. Instead, laws are created by the politicians the public elects to Congress. New gun control laws are difficult to pass because progun organizations such as the NRA give significant donations to politicians. In addition, politicians are motivated to support the NRA because they want to win the votes of the organization's five million members.[14]

## THE NRA

The NRA is an organization focused on protecting gun rights. The group was founded in 1871 to support hunting and shooting sports and safety. The group began its foray into politics in 1934. Initially, it supported several gun control laws, but that changed in the 1970s when the group created a lobbying arm to campaign for the individual right to own guns for self-defense. Today, the NRA is the nation's most powerful gun lobby, with a larger annual budget than all the gun control organizations put together. As a result, it exerts a strong influence on national politics.

# FROM THE
# HEADLINES

## GUN RIGHTS
## GO TO CHURCH

After a 2017 church shooting in Sutherland Springs, Texas, claimed 26 lives, the Lighthouse Church of God in the town of Mexico, New York, sent a clear message. "We're Locked and Loaded—This Is Not a Gun-Free Zone," read the church's welcome sign.[15] Pastor Ronald Russel allowed attendees to bring concealed weapons to church for years, citing his responsibility to keep his members safe. Choir member Janice Fortino says knowing the congregation is armed makes her feel less vulnerable. "Knowing I'm taken care of and protected is a very good feeling," she said.[16]

Russel is not alone in his gun beliefs. A survey by the Public Religion Research Group—a nonprofit research group that looks into topics that involve culture, religion, and public policy—found that 59 percent of evangelical Christians favor gun rights. Even still, religion professor Gustav Niebuhr at Syracuse University said Russel's teaching on guns in church is unusual. "What you're describing is not in any doctrine," Niebuhr said. However, some Christians promote gun control. Father Gerry Waterman, a Catholic, of Syracuse, New York, is concerned that if he fortifies his church, people won't feel welcome. "I've got to trust God that if I err on the side of welcome, God will protect us," Waterman said.[17]

Crosses for shooting victims were placed near Sutherland Springs' First Baptist Church in Sutherland Springs, Texas.

# CHAPTER SEVEN

# PREVENTING
# SCHOOL
# SHOOTINGS

T hough school shootings are statistically rare, they draw significant media attention because the victims are children. Often, the gunmen are only teens themselves. As a result of these events, much has been done to make US schools safer for students. However, experts don't always agree on the best way to protect children, teachers, and schools.

## HARDEN THE TARGET

After school shootings, school districts and politicians often respond by hardening the target. This means fortifying the school by modifying the school building

On the nineteenth anniversary of the Columbine shooting, a group of Oregon students participated in a gun control rally.

to prevent a shooter from entering. It also means changing school policies to make the school a less attractive target.

Hardening the school can involve adding security features such as cameras, automatic door-locking systems, and metal detectors. The property itself can be hardened by adding fencing around the school and redirecting access to the building through a central, well-monitored front entrance. Students and staff can be trained on how to respond to a shooting with school-wide lockdown procedures and emergency training programs. And schools can protect themselves by adding armed police officers, often called school resource officers, to monitor the school campus. After the MSD High School shooting, national leaders even debated whether teachers should be trained to carry guns.

## KIDS MORE LIKELY TO BE SHOT OUTSIDE OF SCHOOL

There are about 55 million schoolchildren in the United States. Based on data collected since the 1992–1993 school year, about ten children die each year from being shot at school.[1] In contrast, children are much more likely to be shot in the home or in the community. A 2017 study published in the American Academy of Pediatrics' journal found that approximately 1,300 children die from gunshot wounds each year. The majority of these deaths are homicides and suicides, with approximately 6 percent being accidental shootings.[2]

Some schools have students walk through a metal detector as a safety measure.

Not everyone believes hardening a school is the best approach. Some experts worry that making schools into fortresses actually makes students feel less safe. "Filling schools with metal detectors, surveillance cameras, police officers and gun-wielding teachers tells students that schools are scary, dangerous, and violent places—places where violence is expected to occur," explained professors Bryan Warnick, Benjamin A. Johnson, and Sam Rocha in a joint article.[3]

In addition, hardening schools can be a challenge because of the high cost of remodeling buildings, training staff, and hiring security personnel. As a result, school

## SCHOOLGUARD APP

Makers of the SchoolGuard mobile phone app aimed to improve police response to school shootings. The app acts as a panic button that any school staff member can activate with his or her phone. Once activated, the system will send alerts to staff in the school as well as to all on- or off-duty police officers in the area. Law enforcement will get the notification on its own app, called Hero911. The app also generates a map of the school with the locations of people inside. Seconds are precious in any mass shooting, and the app's creators hope that faster responses will mean more lives saved.

districts may not be able to afford upgrades to security. Also, there is not always enough research to prove the effectiveness of one security measure over another, making it hard for officials to decide how to best spend their money.

## CREATING SOFT SCHOOLS

Instead of hardening schools, some experts believe schools need to become softer. They argue that a soft school is safer because it is focused on the social and emotional well-being of students. Students who feel welcome, accepted, and involved in school are much less likely to act violently.

One feature that makes schools soft is intentional education around mental health topics such as bullying and suicide prevention. One educational program is the LifeSkills Program, which educates students on topics such

Students who tell teachers about a potential danger can help prevent a serious situation.

as dealing with anxiety and violence in the media. This program has been proven to reduce violence and other problematic behaviors in at-risk students.

Another feature of a soft school is an atmosphere where students feel safe to report potential threats to teachers or administrators. In California, a 2013–2015 survey found that 20 percent of middle and high school students saw a weapon at school during the year.[4] Students who had good relationships with adults at the school were more likely to tell an authority about the weapon.

Another practice commonly used in soft schools is a threat assessment. This procedure was adopted from the Secret Service and is mandatory in Virginia. It is also used in several other states. When a student is identified as a threat to himself or others, a team from the school, including administrators and a school resource officer, meet to discuss the threat and steps needed to keep the student and school safe. If necessary, the school will then notify law enforcement and parents and take measures to protect potential victims.

## GUN-FREE ZONES

Federal laws prohibit firearms in or around schools. In addition, cities and states designate certain public spaces, such as libraries or parks, as gun-free zones. This means no civilian guns are allowed, even for people with a conceal-and-carry permit. The aim is to protect children and citizens from gun violence. Some people argue gun-free zones attract mass shooters because the shooter knows he will not encounter armed civilians. However, according to research collected by *Mother Jones*, mass shooters do not target gun-free zones. "Among the 62 mass shootings during the last 30 years that we studied, not a single case includes evidence that the killer chose to target a place because it banned guns," explained journalist Mark Follman in 2013.[5] Even when the shooting happened in a gun-free zone, Follman argues, the location was selected for another reason, such as a grudge against former employers.

## REPORTING POTENTIAL SHOOTERS

Soft schools work hard to identify potential threats before they become violent events. In the Know the Signs Program— created through a partnership with researchers and Sandy Hook Promise, an advocacy group that aims to educate the public on how to prevent school shootings—students and adults around the country are being trained on how to identify a shooter. The theory behind the program is that mass shootings and other violent events don't happen spontaneously. Instead, shooters typically exhibit identifiable warning signs in the months or weeks before they snap. By training people to look for these warning signs and report them to authorities, citizens can prevent acts of violence, and potential perpetrators can get the help they often need.

## POTENTIAL SCHOOL SHOOTER THWARTED

In 2018, a potential school shooter was thwarted by Marino Chavez at El Camino High School in Southern California. The attentive security guard overheard a 17-year-old boy threaten to open fire at the school only two days after the MSD High School shooting. The threat resulted from an argument with a teacher about the student's use of headphones, which were not allowed in class. Police obtained a warrant and searched the boy's home, finding several guns plus a stash of ammunition. They arrested the student for making threatening comments.

First, the Know the Signs Program says people should notice how individuals talk and act in regard to guns. Shooters often exhibit an extreme fascination with firearms. They may talk about guns frequently or draw

Checking students' backpacks is one security measure some schools take.

or post pictures of them. The may also study how to use guns and show an unhealthy obsession with other mass shooting events. These individuals often have easy, unrestricted access to firearms and brag about that access.

In addition, several behaviors signal a person may be about to snap. Potential shooters often overreact or act out aggressively to seemingly minor conflicts. Their response, in other words, is out of proportion to the situation. Individuals are also at risk for becoming violent if they have a history of being bullied and a real or perceived sense that they are rejected or don't fit in with the group. Other at-risk behaviors include violent gestures, such as making a shooting sign with their hand, a lack of ambition, and a sudden drop in academic or athletic achievement.

If people notice concerning behavior, they can report it to local law enforcement or the FBI. People who are afraid to share information with authorities can call an anonymous hotline. For example, in Colorado, any concerned citizen can anonymously report suspicious or threatening behavior on the Safe2Tell hotline or website. These tips are then funneled to school officials or law enforcement agencies who can investigate and intervene if necessary. In Michigan, a similar program, called Okay2Say, has successfully intervened in instances of bullying, suicide, and threats of violence to others.

Though much work has been done since the Columbine shooting to make schools safer, experts continue to disagree on the best way to protect students at school. Some schools choose to harden the target by increasing security. Others choose to soften their school by focusing on school climate and identifying potential threats. Some schools do a combination of both. But whichever approach officials choose, the goal is the same: to keep students safe.

# CHAPTER EIGHT

# SURVIVING A
# MASS
# SHOOTING

Though mass shootings account for a small fraction of all fatalities in the United States, they cause a lot of public anxiety. A 2017 Gallup poll found that four in ten Americans fear that they or someone they love will be a victim of a mass shooting.[1] New laws and policies could go a long way toward preventing mass shootings. School safety measures and emotional health programs can protect children and the community. In addition, individual citizens can take steps to deter the next mass shooter before a rampage begins. And if individuals are ever unfortunate enough

Some students are taught how to block classroom doors with furniture in the event of a school lockdown.

to experience one of these rare events, experts offer advice on how to make it out alive.

# SITUATIONAL AWARENESS

Most Americans have not been taught what to do if they are in an active shooter event. However, several organizations are trying to change that by providing the public with relevant information on what to do. The US Department of Homeland Security (DHS) has coined the phrase "Run, Hide, Fight" to describe what people should do if caught in a shooting.[2] Other experts such as Gregory Shaffer, a former FBI agent and founder of Shaffer Security Group, remind the public that the necessary actions are not always so simple.

## RESEARCHERS AIM TO END GUN TRAGEDIES

Thirty-one-year-old Yifan Zhang was inspired to enter the field of gun research after the Sandy Hook school shooting. "I have a son who just turned 1. When I think about what I will need to teach him about protecting himself, I think about that school shooting," she said. According to longtime gun researcher Garen Wintemute, there has been a new wave of interest in gun research as mass shootings have become deadlier. Researchers from a variety of fields are joining private or state-funded groups to try and answer some of the biggest gun-safety questions. They hope that by studying big questions like "Are you more or less likely to die if you own a firearm?" they will be able to influence public policy and save lives.[3]

According to Shaffer, the first step to escaping a mass shooting is always to be aware of the surroundings. He encourages people to pay attention to others nearby and be cautious if someone appears out of place. A man standing alone in a crowded theater, wearing oversized clothes when it's hot outside, is one example. "I'm not saying he's up to no good, but you should take another look," Shaffer says.[4]

Former British military officer John Geddes also encourages situational awareness practices. In his book *Be a Hero*, which is about how to survive a mass shooting, Geddes suggests keeping track of exits and fire extinguishers when in a building and always sitting near the door in restaurants and movie theaters. These actions, he says, help create options in the event of an attack.

Many people who survive mass shootings say they first thought the gunshots were fireworks or construction noise.

"MILITARY PERSONNEL, LAW ENFORCEMENT OFFICERS, AND EXPERIENCED MEDIA CORRESPONDENTS ARE AMONG THOSE PROFESSIONALS WHO DO A RUNNING INTERNAL ASSESSMENT OF THEIR SURROUNDINGS INSTINCTIVELY AND UNCONSCIOUSLY. SO DO CRIMINALS AND TERRORISTS. GET USED TO DOING THE SAME."[5]

**—JOHN GEDDES, AUTHOR OF THE BOOK *BE A HERO***

As a result, Shaffer says it's important to quickly assume the sounds are gunfire and act accordingly. Seconds are precious in a shooting event, and responding immediately can make the difference between escaping and becoming a victim.

## RUN, HIDE, FIGHT, AND MORE

If a shooter does open fire, Geddes advises people stay calm, stay aware of the shooter, stay out of the shooter's field of vision, and then run. As with the advice from DHS, Geddes says getting away from the shooter is essential, which is why it's so important to know the location of the nearest exit. However, he warns people to not blindly follow others as they flee: calculating shooters can booby-trap common exits, creating even more casualties.

Safety expert James Hamilton says running is also important for another reason, explaining, "I've been shooting weapons for over 30 years, and it's extremely difficult to hit a moving target. It's far easier to hit a stationary one."[7] If the shooter seems to be following, Geddes suggests creating a distraction, such as throwing tables and chairs in the shooter's path, if possible. "Seconds count during an attack and if you keep shaving seconds off the killer's effective firing time, you are robbing him of victims," Geddes says.[8]

If escape is not an option, Geddes suggests taking cover. He reminds readers that because bullets travel in a straight line, it's important to stay out of the line of

Law enforcement officials visit schools to practice safety drills with students and teachers.

fire. However, Shaffer warns that hiding can leave a person vulnerable—like a sitting duck. If people are hiding in a room, Shaffer suggests turning off the lights, silencing cell phones, and then locking or barricading the door, making it as hard as possible for the shooter to enter. Geddes says janitor's closets and kitchens are especially good hiding places because they have the potential to contain items, such as cleaning chemicals or makeshift weapons, that could be used in self-defense if necessary.

If the shooter is able to enter the room, individuals may be forced to fight. In that case, nearby items can be used to distract or attack. Fire extinguishers can be used to disorient a shooter. A cup of hot coffee, a pen, or a broken chair leg can be used as a makeshift weapon. As is taught in self-defense courses, people can use body parts such as elbows, knees, and hands to apply strong force to the attacker's sensitive areas such as eyes, throat, or groin. If possible, people should act together. A group has a better opportunity of disorienting and overtaking a shooter. Geddes reminds people that they can legally attack the assailant until he is no longer a threat, but they can't use deadly force once he has been subdued.

Finally, once the threat has been neutralized, it's important to treat the wounded. A person trained in CPR can help victims keep breathing until medical assistance arrives. The other main treatment concern is to stop any bleeding. Wounds should be cleaned if possible, and clothing can be applied with pressure to stop blood flow. If the bleeding is excessive, a belt or purse strap can be used as a tourniquet.

Though the likelihood of ever being involved in an active shooter event is very slim, knowing the best thing to do in that instant can help individuals save themselves and those around them. "Not knowing what to do is what generates the greatest fear," says Shaffer. "Having the knowledge can give you a sense of calm."[9]

# FROM THE
# HEADLINES

## BYSTANDERS TAKE DOWN SHOOTER AT GIFFORDS RALLY

On January 8, 2011, US representative Gabrielle Giffords was speaking at a political rally in her home state of Arizona when she was shot and critically injured. The 22-year-old gunman then began shooting into the crowd, killing and wounding several others. That's when fast-acting bystanders jumped into action. First, an unknown assailant smashed the gunman in the back with a folding chair. Then retired army colonel Bill Badger grabbed the shooter and forced him to the ground. Patricia Maisch heard someone shout "Get his magazine" and grabbed the magazine from the shooter's hand while someone else took his gun.[10] Another bystander, Roger Salzgeber, helped Badger pin down the shooter while Maisch held his ankles.

Inside a nearby store, Joe Zamudio heard the gunshots. He rushed out with his conceal-and-carry handgun in his pocket. When he saw an older man holding the shooter's gun, Zamudio

Gabrielle Giffords works hard to stop gun violence.

guessed he was the shooter and took aim. Fortunately, he didn't pull the trigger. Instead, a gut feeling prompted Zamudio to rush forward. The bystanders around him shouted that the man pinned to the ground was the real shooter. Meanwhile, Giffords's intern Daniel Hernandez applied pressure to her wounds and helped keep her alert until help arrived. Giffords survived the encounter. Though six people lost their lives that day, the toll could have been much worse if it weren't for a handful of civilian heroes.[11]

# FORGIVE, AND ADVOCATE

The effects of a mass shooting are often greater than people realize. Researchers and reporters usually focus on the number of people killed or injured in a shooting. But they don't quantify the number of bystanders who may have escaped yet bear emotional scars from the tragedy. A study by the *Washington Post* tried to count the number of students who have experienced a school shooting. By researching incidents since Columbine in 1999 until 2018, they estimate approximately 187,000 students have been at school when a gunman opened fire.[1] In addition, there is no tracker that counts the number of

Part of the healing process is mourning the people who were killed.

family members and friends devastated when someone they love is critically injured or killed. Yet the emotional cost on the victims' loved ones can be devastating.

As a result of these tragedies, some victims, witnesses, and their loved ones struggle with physical or mental health issues for the rest of their lives. Others learn how to cope, move forward, and forgive. Some even turn into advocates, striving to make sure no one else has to suffer what they have endured.

## ORLANDO MURALS SHOW SUPPORT

Gay rights can be a heated issue among politicians in Orlando, Florida. But a year after the 2016 Orlando nightclub shooting, the response from the community was nothing but compassionate. A tangible reminder of the community's support was the rainbow-colored murals that sprang up around the city. One such mural was across the street from the nightclub, on the wall of a bagel shop. The restaurant's parking lot was used to treat victims after the shooting, and police told the manager one person even died there. In response, the store commissioned a mural showing four hands spelling the word *love* along with 49 flowers, one for each victim.[2]

## COLUMBINE SURVIVORS

Although the students who lived through the Columbine shooting are adults, many still live with physical and emotional scars from the tragedy. Samantha Haviland survived the shooting. But she didn't realize how much the shooting had affected her until almost nine years later, when a school she was working in at the time had a lockdown drill. Her ensuing panic attack inspired her to get counseling. Though she still had flashbacks and nightmares of the event, she's told her story so many times that it doesn't tear her apart anymore. Haviland became the director of counseling for Denver Public Schools and works hard to ensure that students get the mental health help they need.

Austin Eubanks is another Columbine survivor. He watched his best friend die in front of him, then he escaped with gunshot wounds in his hand and knees. As a result of his injuries, he was prescribed painkillers, which led to a drug and alcohol addiction. He abused substances to try and mask the emotional pain from the shooting. After 12 years of addiction, he got sober and began working at an addiction treatment center in Steamboat Springs, Colorado. Eubanks gives advice to other shooting survivors. "In order to heal

## MOTHER OF THE COLUMBINE SHOOTER

For years, Sue Klebold, the mother of Columbine shooter Dylan, kept silent. In 2017, she said she knew people were judging her as a mother and were questioning how she didn't know her son was capable of such violence. Her own emotional pain led to panic attacks, physical illness, and mental health issues. Knowing she needed to heal, she pulled together her memories and reached out to experts, trying to figure out what went wrong with her son. She even wrote a book, *A Mother's Reckoning*, sharing her story in candid detail.

Years after the Columbine shooting, survivors continued to visit the grave sites of their classmates.

emotional pain, you have to feel it," he says. "You want to feel better immediately, [but] you have to have the courage to sit in and feel it, and if you can do that long enough, you will come out on the other side."[3]

## FAMILIES PUSH FOR CHANGE AND FORGIVENESS

In the Sandy Hook shooting, 20 of the victims were six or seven years old.[4] This loss left families and a community reeling. "The tragedy impacted every aspect of my life," said Nicole Hockley, whose son, Dylan, was killed. "Not only because of the obvious absence of my son but because of the constant hole inside me that can never be filled." Hockley and several other parents banded together to form the advocacy group Sandy Hook Promise. "We can allow this event to change and define us. Or we can be the ones who change first and take action and define what happens next," Hockley said.[5]

Another Sandy Hook parent-turned-activist, Alissa Parker, cofounded the organization Safe and Sound Schools, which provides crisis response, support, and recovery training resources to schools. She also wrote a book, *An Unseen Angel*, about her journey through the grief of losing her daughter Emilie. Parker relied on her Christian faith to help her learn how to forgive the shooter for killing her daughter. She writes candidly about how she learned to rely on God to let go of her pain. "As I made this decision, a burden so deep and so heavy it had nearly crushed me was lifted from me. . . . I had learned it was possible to forgive Adam Lanza and that the first step for me was to choose to simply let go."[6]

Victims of church shootings also rely on their faith to help them process and move past the tragedy. Charleston, South Carolina, was the setting for a 2015 shooting that

Thousands of shoes were placed outside the US Capitol building in 2018. The shoes represented children who died because of gun violence since the Sandy Hook shooting.

killed nine people.[7] The shooter, Dylann Roof, a 21-year-old white male fueled by racial hatred, entered Emanuel African Methodist Episcopal Church, an African American church, and opened fire on a prayer meeting. Among those killed were several church leaders, including the pastor and State Senator Clementa C. Pinckney. For some people affected by the tragedy, forgiveness came quickly. At the bond hearing for the shooter, held only a few days later, church and community members gathered and repeatedly told the shooter, "I forgive you." Others confess that though they know they are called by God to forgive, it took them longer. "With me, forgiveness is a process," said Polly Sheppard, who survived the shooting.[8]

## TEENS IGNITE A MOVEMENT

Survivors of the MSD High School shooting responded to the tragedy like others before them—they took on an activist role. The key difference was that these activists were teenagers. Some of them were still too young to vote. But that didn't stop them from spreading their #NeverAgain campaign across the United States and the world. They used social media to ignite a firestorm with their call for lawmakers to protect the nation's children by changing gun laws to prevent school shootings.

On March 9, 2018, Florida lawmakers passed legislation that banned bump stocks, increased the minimum age for gun purchases, allowed guns to be taken away from those with mental illness, and created a three-day waiting period for gun purchases. The purpose of a waiting period is to deter someone from buying a gun in the heat of the moment and

"IS IT POSSIBLE THAT WE CAN BE THE GENERATION THAT MAKES THE CHANGES TO GUN LAWS? I WOULD LOVE THAT. BUT IT'S HARD TO TELL THE FUTURE. I WISH I HAD A CRYSTAL BALL."[9]

—BRANDON ABZUG, A SURVIVOR OF THE MSD HIGH SCHOOL SHOOTING

# MORE TO THE
# STORY

## MARCH FOR OUR LIVES

Children and adults throughout the world gathered at a total of 846 March for Our Lives rallies on March 24, 2018. Some carried posters with slogans such as "Arms are for hugging, not killing" and "Protect kids, not guns." Some carried photos of friends killed by gun violence. And they all listened to passionate speakers who demanded change. At the rally in Washington, DC, several MSD High School survivors gave speeches. "Fight for your lives, before it's someone else's job," high school senior Emma González told the crowd. She also called for six minutes and 20 seconds of silence—the amount of time it took the shooter to take the lives of 17 of her classmates and teachers. Yolanda Renee King, the nine-year-old granddaughter of Martin Luther King Jr., and Coretta Scott King also made an appearance at the DC rally. Yolanda told the audience, "I have a dream that enough is enough. That this should be a gun-free world. Period." Children also came out in droves for the rally. One fourth grader from nearby Arlington, Virginia, stood with protesters and carried a sign that read, "We may be small but we have a voice!"[10]

immediately using it to commit a crime. On March 14—one month after the shooting—hundreds of thousands of schoolchildren across the nation participated in school walkouts to protest mass violence. And on March 24, MSD High School students coordinated the March for Our Lives rally in Washington, DC, which included hundreds of satellite protests in all US states and on every continent—even Antarctica.

What started as a grassroots, student-led movement gained international attention. And even if the MSD High School students didn't see national gun legislation right away, they were determined to keep fighting. They hoped to create a culture of teens who advocate for youth issues and who sway public policy with their vote. And they hoped to embolden the next generation of politicians with the power to solve the problems of school safety and gun violence.

# ESSENTIAL
# FACTS

## MAJOR EVENTS

- People consider a shooting at the University of Texas, Austin, as the first modern mass shooting. On August 1, 1966, a former marine killed his wife and mother, then took a small arsenal of firearms to the top of a prominent tower on the college campus. He killed 17 people and injured many more.

- The school shooting at Columbine High School in Littleton, Colorado, captured national attention for months. On April 20, 1999, two high school seniors stormed the school and killed 13 people. This was the first school shooting to receive widespread media coverage.

- The deadliest mass shooting in US history as of mid-2018 took place during a concert in Las Vegas, Nevada. On October 1, 2017, a 64-year-old gunman barricaded himself in his room at the Mandalay Bay Resort and Casino and rained bullets into the crowd below. Fifty-eight people were killed.

## KEY PLAYERS

- The National Rifle Association is the major gun-rights advocacy group in the United States. It supports gun safety education and champions the rights of American citizens to own firearms for protection.

- Several groups promote gun control and advocate to end gun violence. The Brady Campaign to End Gun Violence champions changes to gun laws, such as requiring universal background checks. Another group is Sandy Hook Promise, which works to prevent school shootings.

## IMPACT ON SOCIETY

Mass shootings kill and injure innocent people. These events can also create physical and emotional trauma for victims. Mass shootings spark heated debates over gun control in the United States, with strong opinions from all sides.

## QUOTE

"We Americans are not an inherently more violent people than folks in other countries. . . . The main difference that sets our nation apart, what makes us so susceptible to so many mass shootings, is that we don't do enough—we don't take the basic common-sense actions to keep guns out of the hands of criminals and dangerous people. What's different in America is that it's easy to get your hands on a gun."

—President Barack Obama, 2013

# GLOSSARY

### ACTIVIST
A person who campaigns to bring about political or social change.

### BUMP STOCK
An attachment that allows a semiautomatic rifle to shoot bullets faster than it could have otherwise.

### EPIDEMIC
The widespread occurrence of something negative.

### INDISCRIMINATE
Random or without careful judgment.

### LGBTQ
An acronym used to describe nonheterosexual people: lesbian, gay, bisexual, transgender, and queer or questioning.

## MAGAZINE

A compartment of a gun where the bullets are held.

## MASCULINITY

Qualities that are commonly associated with men.

## PERPETRATOR

Someone who is responsible for an act.

## REGISTRY

An official list kept by a government or organization.

## SEMIAUTOMATIC WEAPON

A weapon that fires a single shot with every pull of the trigger and automatically reloads from a magazine between shots.

## TRAUMA

An emotionally disturbing or distressing event.

# ADDITIONAL
# RESOURCES

## SELECTED BIBLIOGRAPHY

Duwe, Grant. *Mass Murder in the United States: A History*. McFarland, 2007.

Klarevas, Louis. *Rampage Nation: Securing America from Mass Shootings*. Prometheus, 2016.

Schildkraut, Jaclyn. *Mass Shootings: Media, Myths, and Realities*. Praeger, 2016.

## FURTHER READINGS

Harris, Duchess. *The Right to Bear Arms*. Abdo, 2018.

Lusted, Marcia Amidon. *Florida School Shooting*. Abdo, 2019.

Owings, Lisa. *The Newtown School Shooting*. Abdo, 2014.

# ONLINE RESOURCES

**Booklinks**
**NONFICTION NETWORK**
**FREE!** ONLINE NONFICTION RESOURCES

To learn more about mass shootings in America, visit **abdobooklinks.com**. These links are routinely monitored and updated to provide the most current information available.

# MORE INFORMATION

For more information on this subject, contact or visit the following organizations:

Brady Campaign to Prevent Gun Violence
840 First Street NE, Suite 400
Washington, DC 20002
202-370-8100
bradycampaign.org
The Brady Campaign to Prevent Gun Violence contains information and research about gun violence, and the organization aims to cut gun deaths in half by 2025.

Everytown for Gun Safety
P.O. Box 4184
New York, NY 10163
646-324-8250
everytown.org
Everytown for Gun Safety provides support for shooting victims and works for gun control.

# SOURCE NOTES

## CHAPTER 1. WHAT IS A MASS SHOOTING?

1. Alene Tchekmedyian. "These Are the Victims of the Rancho Tehama Shooting Rampage." *Los Angeles Times*, 16 Nov. 2017, latimes.com. Accessed 1 Aug. 2018.

2. "Quick Look: 220 Active Shooter Incidents in the United States from 2000–2016." *FBI*, n.d., fbi.gov. Accessed 1 Aug. 2018.

3. Eric Westervelt. "Quick Acting School Staff in California Avert a Sandy Hook Massacre." *NPR*, 16 Nov. 2017, npr.org. Accessed 1 Aug. 2018.

4. Sonali Kohli. "Why No Children Died during the Rancho Tehama School Shooting." *LA Times*, 16 Nov. 2017, latimes.com. Accessed 1 Aug. 2018.

5. Chris Wilson. "Why Are There So Many Conflicting Numbers on Mass Shootings?" *Time*, 1 Oct. 2017, time.com. Accessed 1 Aug. 2018.

6. Wilson, "Why Are There So Many Conflicting Numbers on Mass Shootings?"

7. "Active Shooter Incidents in the United States between 2014–2015." *FBI*, n.d., fbi.gov. Accessed 1 Aug. 2018.

8. Josh Sanburn. "Why the FBI Report that Mass Shootings Are Up Can Be Misleading." *Time*, 26 Sept. 2014, time.com. Accessed 1 Aug. 2018.

9. Chris Nichols. "How Is Mass Shooting Defined?" *Politifact*, 4 Oct. 2017, polifact.com. Accessed 1 Aug. 2018.

10. Nichols, "How Is Mass Shooting Defined?"

11. Mark Follman, et al. "US Mass Shootings 1982–2018: Data from Mother Jones' Investigation." *Mother Jones*, 10 Mar. 2018, motherjones.com. Accessed 1 Aug. 2018.

12. Sherry L. Murphy, et al. "Deaths: Final Data for 2015." *CDC*, 27 Nov. 2017, cdc.gov. Accessed 1 Aug. 2018.

13. Abbey Oldham. "2015: The Year of Mass Shootings." *PBS*, 1 Jan. 2016, pbs.org. Accessed 1 Aug. 2018.

## CHAPTER 2. THE HISTORY OF MASS SHOOTINGS

1. "Fourteen Persons Wounded." *Daily Alta California*, 31 Mar. 1891, cdnc.ucr.edu. Accessed 1 Aug. 2018.

2. "Mass Public Shootings on the Rise. But Why?" *NBC News*, 21 Apr. 2007, nbcnews.com. Accessed 1 Aug. 2018.

3. Lorraine Boissoneault. "The 1927 Bombing That Remains America's Deadliest School Massacre." *Smithsonian*, 18 May 2017, smithsonianmag.com. Accessed 1 Aug. 2018.

4. "Beginning of an Era: The 1966 University of Texas Clock Tower Shooting." *NBC News*, 31 July 2016, nbcnews.com. Accessed 1 Aug. 2018.

5. Grant Duwe. *Mass Murder in the United States: A History*. McFarland, 2007. 63.

6. Jaclyn Schildkraut. *Mass Shootings: Media, Myths, and Realities*. Praeger, 2016. 36.

7. Bonnie Berkowitz, et al. "The Terrible Numbers That Grow with Each Mass Shooting." *Washington Post*, 14 Mar. 2018, washingtonpost.com. Accessed 1 Aug. 2018.

8. "Columbine Shooting." *History*, n.d., history.com. Accessed 1 Aug. 2018.

9. Schildkraut, *Mass Shootings*, 38.

10. Schildkraut, *Mass Shootings*, 43.

11. Schildkraut, *Mass Shootings*, 43.

12. Berkowitz et al. "The Terrible Numbers That Grow with Each Mass Shooting."

13. "Sandy Hook Shooting: What Happened?" *CNN*, n.d., cnn.com. Accessed 1 Aug. 2018.

14. Mike Schneider. "Report: After Pulse Nightclub Massacre in Orlando, Police Training Needs Changes." *Naples Daily News*, 27 May 2017, naplesnews.com. Accessed 1 Aug. 2018.

15. Mark Follman, et al. "US Mass Shootings, 1982–2018: Data from Mother Jones' Investigation." *Mother Jones*, 28 June 2018, motherjones.com. Accessed 1 Aug. 2018.

## CHAPTER 3. AN AMERICAN PROBLEM?

1. "Remarks by the President at the Memorial Service for Victims of the Navy Yard Shooting." *White House*, 22 Sept. 2013, obamawhitehouse.archives.gov. Accessed 1 Aug. 2018.

2. Kara Fox. "How US Gun Culture Compares with the World in Five Charts." *CNN*, 9 Mar. 2018, cnn.com. Accessed 1 Aug. 2018.

3. Darla Cameron and Samuel Granados. "Mass Shootings: How US Gun Culture Compares with the Rest of the World." *Washington Post*, 15 Feb. 2018, washingtonpost.com. Accessed 1 Aug. 2018.

4. Samantha Michaels. "The United States Has Had More Mass Shootings Than Any Other Country." *Mother Jones*, 23 Aug. 2015, motherjones.com. Accessed 1 Aug. 2018.

5. "A Look Back at the Norway Massacre." *CBS News*, 18 Feb. 2013, cbsnews.com. Accessed 1 Aug. 2018.

6. Cameron and Granados, "Mass Shootings."

7. Fox, "How US Gun Culture Compares with the World in Five Charts."

8. Fox, "How US Gun Culture Compares with the World in Five Charts."

9. Clifton Leaf. "How Australia All But Ended Gun Violence." *Fortune*, 20 Feb. 2018, fortune.com. Accessed 1 Aug. 2018.

10. Helena Bachmann. "The Swiss Difference: A Gun Culture That Works." *Time*, 20 Dec. 2012, world.time.com. Accessed 1 Aug. 2018.

11. Bachmann, "The Swiss Difference."

## CHAPTER 4. PROFILE OF A SHOOTER

1. John Haltiwanger. "White Men Have Committed More Mass Shootings Than Any Other Group." *Newsweek*, 21 Oct. 2017, newsweek.com. Accessed 1 Aug. 2018.

2. Polly DeFrank and Elizabeth Chuck. "Wife in San Bernardino Shooting Joins Small List of Women Mass Killers." *NBC News*, 3 Dec. 2015, nbcnews.com. Accessed 1 Aug. 2018.

3. "1,077 People Have Been Killed in Mass Shootings since a 1966 Incident at the University of Texas." *Lily*, 15 Feb. 2015, thelily.com. Accessed 1 Aug. 2018.

4. Bonnie Berkowitz, et al. "The Terrible Numbers That Grow with Each Mass Shooting." *Washington Post*, 14 Mar. 2018, washingtonpost.com. Accessed 1 Aug. 2018.

5. Jeff Daniels. "Definition of What's Actually an Assault Weapon Is a Contentious Issue." *CNBC*, 21 Feb. 2018, cnbc.com. Accessed 1 Aug. 2018.

6. Laura Kiesel. "Don't Blame Mental Illness for Mass Shootings; Blame Men." *Politico*, 17 Jan. 2018, politico.com. Accessed 1 Aug. 2018.

7. Grant Duwe and Michael Rocque. "Actually There Is a Clear Link Between Mass Shootings and Mental Illness." *Los Angeles Times*, 23 Feb. 2018, latimes.com. Accessed 1 Aug. 2018.

8. Daniel Victor. "Mass Shooters Are All Different Except for One Thing: They're All Men." *New York Times*, 17 Feb. 2018, nytimes.com. Accessed 1 Aug. 2018.

9. Berkowitz et al. "The Terrible Numbers That Grow with Each Mass Shooting."

10. Ann O'Neill. "Theater Shooter Holms Gets 12 Life Sentences, Plus 3,318 Years." *CNN*, 27 Aug. 2015, cnn.com. Accessed 1 Aug. 2018.

11. Jamie Ducharme. "Stop Blaming School Shootings on Mental Illness, Top Psychologist Warns." *Time*, 16 Feb. 2018, time.com. Accessed 1 Aug. 2018.

## CHAPTER 5. US CULTURE AND MASS SHOOTERS

1. Tony Rom. "President to Meet with Video Game Executives and Critics about Violence." *Washington Post*, 8 Mar. 2018, washingtonpost.com. Accessed 1 Aug. 2018.

2. Laurel Wamsley and Richard Gonzales. "17 People Died in the Parkland Shooting. Here Are Their Names." *NPR*, 15 Feb. 2018, npr.org. Accessed 1 Aug. 2018.

3. Daniel Arkin. "Here's What We Know about the Links between Video Games and Violence." *NBC News*, 2 Mar. 2018, nbcnews.com. Accessed 1 Aug. 2018.

4. Anna Werner. "80 Percent of Shooters Showed No Interest in Video Games, Researchers Say." *CBS News*, 8 Mar. 2018, cbsnews.com. Accessed 1 Aug. 2018.

# SOURCE NOTES
## CONTINUED

5. David Anderson and Steven Kovach. "Stop Blaming Violent Video Games for Mass Shootings." *Business Insider*, 10 Apr. 2018, businessinsider.com. Accessed 1 Aug. 2018.

6. Simon Parkin. "Donald Trump Takes On Non-Existent Link between Violent Video Games and Mass Shootings." *New Yorker*, 8 Mar. 2018, newyorker.com. Accessed 1 Aug. 2018.

7. Jennifer Wright. "Men Are Responsible for Mass Shootings: How Toxic Masculinity Is Killing Us." *Harper's Bazaar*, 16 Feb. 2018, harpersbazaar.com. Accessed 1 Aug. 2018.

8. "Arrests by Sex, 2012." *FBI: UCR*, n.d., ucr.fbi.gov. Accessed 1 Aug. 2018.

9. Wright, "Men Are Responsible for Mass Shootings."

10. Derek Thompson. "Mass Shootings in America Are Spreading Like a Disease." *Atlantic*, 6 Nov. 2017, theatlantic.com. Accessed 1 Aug. 2018.

11. Daniella Silva. "Mass Shootings Are Getting Deadlier, Experts Say." *NBC News*, 7 Nov. 2017, nbcnews.com. Accessed 1 Aug. 2018.

12. Bonnie Berkowitz, et al. "The Terrible Numbers That Grow with Each Mass Shooting." *Washington Post*, 14 Mar. 2018, washingtonpost.com. Accessed 1 Aug. 2018.

13. Emily Deruy. "The Warning Signs of a Mass Shooting." *Atlantic*, 2 Dec. 2015, theatlantic.com. Accessed 1 Aug. 2018.

## CHAPTER 6. THE GUN DEBATE

1. AJ Willingham. "27 Words: Deconstructing the Second Amendment." *CNN*, 28 Mar. 2018, cnn.com. Accessed 1 Aug. 2018.

2. Greg St. Martin. "New Study Finds 1 in 5 Gun Owners Obtained Firearm without a Permit." *News@ Northeastern*, 5 Jan. 2017, news.northeastern.edu. Accessed 1 Aug. 2018.

3. Mark Follman and Gavin Aronsen. "'A Killing Machine': Half of All Mass Shooters Used High-Capacity Magazines." *Mother Jones*, 30 Jan. 2013, motherjones.com. Accessed 1 Aug. 2018.

4. "Background Checks." *Brady Campaign*, n.d., bradycampaign.org. Accessed 1 Aug. 2018.

5. "NRA: 'Only Way to Stop a Bad Guy with a Gun Is a Good Guy with a Gun.'" *CBS*, 21 Dec. 2012, washington.cbslocal.com. Accessed 1 Aug. 2018.

6. Max Fischer and Josh Keller. "What Explains U.S. Mass Shootings? International Comparisons Suggest an Answer." *New York Times*, 7 Nov. 2017, nytimes.com. Accessed 1 Aug. 2018.

7. Elspeth Reeve. "Why the NRA Is Still Winning the War on Guns." *Atlantic*, 14 Dec. 2012, theatlantic.com. Accessed 1 Aug. 2018.

8. Tony Romm. "Trump's Meeting with the Video Game Industry to Talk Gun Violence Could Get Ugly." *Washington Post*, 7 Mar. 2018, washingtonpost.com. Accessed 1 Aug. 2018.

9. John R. Lott Jr. "Gun Control Misfires in Europe." *Wall Street Journal*, 30 Apr. 2002, wsj.com. Accessed 1 Aug. 2018.

10. Samantha Raphelson. "How Often Do People Use Guns in Self-Defense?" *NPR*, 13 Apr. 2018, npr.org. Accessed 1 Aug. 2018.

11. "Risks of Having a Gun in the Home." *Brady Center*, n.d., bradycampaign.org. Accessed 1 Aug. 2018.

12. Hilary Brueck and Shayanne Gal. "The US Spends Less on Gun Violence Research Than Nearly Every Other Leading Cause of Death—and That's on Purpose." *Business Insider*, 6 Mar. 2018, businessinsider.com. Accessed 1 Aug. 2018.

13. "U.S. Support for Gun Control Tops 2-1, Highest Ever, Quinnipiac University National Poll Finds; Let Dreamers Stay, 80 Percent of Voters Say." *Quinnipiac University Poll*, 20 Feb. 2018, poll.qu.edu. Accessed 1 Aug. 2018.

14. Anthony Zurcher. "Las Vegas Shooting: Five Reasons US Gun Control Won't Happen." *BBC*, 4 Oct. 2017, bbc.com. Accessed 22 Aug. 2018.

15. Alexis Jones. "In the Great Lakes Town of Mexico, NY, a Pastor Boldly Claims, 'We're Locked and Loaded. This is Not a Gun-Free Zone.'" *Belt Magazine*, 1 Feb. 2018, beltmag.com. Accessed 1 Aug. 2018.

16. Payne Horning. "Armed at Church: Why This Congregation Is 'Not a Gun-Free Zone.'" *NPR*, 8 Apr. 2018, npr.org. Accessed 1 Aug. 2018.

17. Jones, "In the Great Lakes Town of Mexico, NY."

## CHAPTER 7. PREVENTING SCHOOL SHOOTINGS

1. Allie Nicodemo and Lia Petronio. "School Are Safer Than They Were in the 90s, and School Shootings Are Not More Common Than They Used to Be, Researchers Say." *News@Northeastern*, 26 Feb. 2018, news.northeastern.edu. Accessed 1 Aug. 2018.

2. Jacqueline Howard. "Guns Kill Nearly 1,300 US Children Each Year, Study Finds." *CNN*, 19 June 2017, cnn.com. Accessed 1 Aug. 2018.

3. "Why Security Measures Won't Stop School Shootings." *Conversation*, 14 Feb. 2018, theconversation.com. Accessed 1 Aug. 2018.

4. Gregory Austin, et al. "School Climate, Substance Use, and Student Well-Being in California, 2013–2015." *California Healthy Kids Survey*, n.d., surveydata.wested.org. Accessed 1 Aug. 2018.

5. Mark Follman. "No, Mass Shooters Do Not Target Gun-Free Zones." *Mother Jones*, 1 Mar. 2018, motherjones.com. Accessed 1 Aug. 2018.

## CHAPTER 8. SURVIVING A MASS SHOOTING

1. Frank Newport. "Four in 10 Americans Fear Being a Victim of a Mass Shooting." *Gallup*, 18 Oct. 2017, news.gallup.com. Accessed 1 Aug. 2018.

2. "Active Shooter Pocket Card." *U.S. Department of Homeland Security*, n.d., dhs.gov. Accessed 1 Aug. 2018.

3. William Wan. "Tenacious New Gun Researchers Are Determined to Break Cycle of Mass Shootings." *Chicago Tribune*, 25 Mar. 2018, chicagotribune.com. Accessed 1 Aug. 2018.

4. Zahra Barnes. "Mass Shootings Are Actually Pretty Rare, But Here's What to Do If You're Ever in One." *Self*, 24 Mar. 2018, self.com. Accessed 1 Aug. 2018.

5. John Geddes. *Be A Hero: The Essential Survival Guide to Active Shooter Events*. Skyhorse, 2017. 24.

6. Cade Metz. "How Facebook Is Transforming Disaster Response." *Wired*, 10 Nov. 2016, wired.com. Accessed 1 Aug. 2018.

7. Barnes, "Mass Shootings Are Actually Pretty Rare."

8. Geddes, *Be A Hero*, 52.

9. Barnes, "Mass Shootings Are Actually Pretty Rare."

10. Geddes, *Be A Hero*, 115–117.

11. Geddes, *Be A Hero*, 115–117.

## CHAPTER 9. HEAL, FORGIVE, AND ADVOCATE

1. Cox Woodrow John and Steven Rich. "Scarred by School Shootings." *Washington Post*, 24 Mar. 2018, washingtonpost.com. Accessed 1 Aug. 2018.

2. John Couwels. "Hearts and Minds Changed." *CNN*, 29 June 2017, cnn.com. Accessed 18 Apr. 2018.

3. Lois Beckett. "Columbine Survivor to Florida Students: 'You Will Come Out on the Other Side.'" *Guardian*, 15 Feb. 2018, theguardian.com. Accessed 1 Aug. 2018.

4. "Connecticut Shooting Fast Facts." *CNN*, 7 Dec. 2017, cnn.com. Accessed 1 Aug. 2018.

5. Nicole Hockley. "Preventing Gun Violence without Just Talking about the Gun." *YouTube*, 4 Feb. 2015, youtube.com. Accessed 1 Aug. 2018.

6. Alissa Parker. *An Unseen Angel: A Mother's Story of Faith, Hope and Healing After Sandy Hook*. Ensign Peak, 2017. 137.

7. Herb Frazier. *We Are Charleston: Tragedy and Triumph at Mother Emanuel*. W Publishing Group, 2016. 164–167.

8. Frazier, *We Are Charleston*, 164–167.

9. Melissa Chan. "Parkland Students on Life after Shooting: 'I Am Not Actually Fine.'" *Time*, 22 Mar. 2018, time.com. Accessed 1 Aug. 2018.

10. Austa Somvichian-Clausen. "Photos from March for Our Lives Events around the Globe." *National Geographic*, 25 Mar. 2018, news.nationalgeographic.com. Accessed 1 Aug. 2018.

# INDEX

# ABOUT THE
# AUTHORS

## DUCHESS HARRIS, JD, PHD

Professor Harris is the chair of the American Studies department at Macalester College and curator of the Duchess Harris Collection of ABDO books. She is the author and coauthor of recently released ABDO books including *Hidden Human Computers: The Black Women of NASA*, *Black Lives Matter*, and *Race and Policing*.

Before working with ABDO, she authored several other books on the topics of race, culture, and American history. She served as an associate editor for *Litigation News*, the American Bar Association Section of Litigation's quarterly flagship publication, and was the first editor in chief of *Law Raza*, an interactive online journal covering race and the law, published at William Mitchell College of Law. She has earned a PhD in American Studies from the University of Minnesota and a JD from William Mitchell College of Law.

## JENNIFER SIMMS

Jennifer Simms is a freelance writer and educator. She lives with her family in Boulder, Colorado. *Mass Shootings in America* is her second book for the school and library market.